Cultural diversity

Jean Michel-Baer, Arjo Klamer, David Throsby,
Issiaka-Prosper Lalèyê

With an introduction by
Fiona Bartels-Ellis

Series editor
Rosemary Bechler

First published 2004
British Council
10 Spring Gardens
London SW1A 2BN
www.britishcouncil.org

Cover design by Atelier Works

Contents

Preface
by the Director-General

The British Council seeks to build long-term relationships between people of different cultures. Our currency is trust. The British Council has been a leader in cultural relations since its founding in 1934. In order to celebrate our 70th anniversary, I asked Counterpoint, our think tank on cultural relations, to commission a series of ten sets of essays, each set looking at a central issue from a variety of angles and viewpoints. The issues range from European enlargement to 'Britishness', and from the significance of death to the role of faith and the nature of secularism.

The 34 writers come from all over the world, though at least one in each set is British. Each introduction, with one exception, is written by a member of British Council staff. They testify to the richness of the intellectual and moral resource that the British Council represents.

Our intention is to stimulate debate rather than arrive at consensus. Some essays are controversial. None of them expresses, individually, a British Council viewpoint. They are the work of individual authors of distinction from whom we have sought views. But collectively, they represent something more than the sum of their parts – a commitment to the belief that dialogue is the essential heart of cultural relations.

Dialogue requires and generates trust. The biggest danger in what is often called public diplomacy work is that we simply broadcast views, policies, values and positions. A senior European diplomat recently said at a British Council conference: 'The world is fed up with hearing us talk. What it wants is for us to shut up and listen.' Listening and demonstrating our commitment to the free and creative interplay of ideas is an indispensable pre-condition for building trust.

To build trust we must engage in effective, open dialogue. Increased mutual understanding based on trust, whether we agree or disagree, is a precious outcome.

David Green KCMG

I would like to acknowledge with gratitude the help of the Government of Quebec in conceiving and commissioning this volume in the Counterpoints series.

Introduction

Fiona Bartels-Ellis

The cultural diversity discourse is born out of a struggle with difference; a multifaceted, changing, nuanced struggle. I engaged with it overtly, yet unconsciously, when I came to this country as an eight year old, learning early on, first hand, the deep-seated negative resonance of difference, its intolerance of other experiences, ways of being, world views and physical features. But I also have my dual heritage to thank for a sense of the potential in difference that allows cultural groups not only to coexist but also to enrich each other. The current 'melting pot' has a variety unimaginable in my youth and some of the world's children negotiate their hybrid identities with an ease and joy that I envy.

Cultural diversity has created new possibilities, new conversations within communities as well as between them, but also new and unforeseen challenges: changing national borders, protracted global conflicts based on ethnicity, and the increasing encounter with difference resulting from communications and transport systems of such sophistication that richness and breadth is brought daily into our lives in more ways than we can ever acknowledge. National identities reshaped by wider membership of such bodies as the European Union or the African Union join with generational differences to ensure that the experience of cultural diversity and attitudes towards it are in a constant state of flux. The ensuing politics of recognition, which demand that previously marginalised or suppressed voices be heard, presents yet another layer to consider and respond to at a policy and practice level, and in our interactions with each other. Such factors, as well as the interdependent nature of 21st -century living, keep cultural diversity issues topical as never before.

Within all of these shifting goalposts, there are issues of power – financial, political or other – as reflected in this book in Issiaka-Prosper Lalèyê's discussion of culture as a tradeable commodity, and Arjo Klamer's meditation on cultural value viewed through his economist's lens.

I write here as a staff member of the British Council, an organisation that relies for its success on its ability to nurture relationships out of the rich potential of cultural diversity. The British Council's role is premised on its positive aspects. Colleagues worldwide hold the sense of the rich potential of diversity as a core belief. But we must not become complacent. The comforting sense of reward about what we do, engendered by the intrinsically positive nature of our work – that of creating opportunity, developing and harnessing talent, showcasing and sharing achievement – needs to be kept under constant review, not least in our relationship to power.

Power doesn't always present itself as a visible yoke of oppression. As British Council employees, we are contributors to the progress of UK foreign policy, and our responsibilities necessarily involve us in the practice of a certain cultural hegemony. Hegemony is about dominance; determining what is accepted as *common sense*, and drawing on the strength of our ideology and social institutions to win active consent and legitimacy. It shapes not only our role but how we are with each other. As employees, we can't be held responsible for much of its workings: let's get real – it is more complex and bigger than each one of us. Success depends on economic, cultural and political alliances, in turn determined by the UK's colonial history or its current economic standing.

At the same time, our cultural relations goal requires that we assert our independence, often taking up an 'arms length' position to the other purposes of power. This is not a stance, but a form of action requiring that we challenge the subtle ways in which things are accorded value so that oppression results. It is a challenge that to be effective, requires leadership. But there is a certain kind of action that each one of us can take, simply by being attentive to the power relations and dynamics that are part of the myriad cultural interactions taking place in and out of our offices around the world. I especially stress the individual level because experience tells me that acting within one's locus of control is what cumulatively leads to sustained change. All of us are in a position to question the cultural hegemony that underpins our work, and open up a space for dialogue.

I believe fervently that our considerations of cultural diversity require a meticulous attention to the misuse or abuse of power, so often at the root of the tensions that arise. It will be the careful exercise of power and our navigations around it, that will allow cultural diversity to flourish, and release its positive potential. Jean-Michel Baer, in warning of the strength and determination that may be needed to offset future threats to democracy, underscores this imperative. He reminds us that the richness and multiplicity of the 'human mosaic', and the benefit that we derive simply from the joyful knowledge of its existence, which David Throsby likens to the intrinsic value of biodiversity – is something we cannot leave to chance. Here in the British Council we know that in many ways, the more mutual these relationships are, the more challenges we confront, not only in terms of addressing ourselves to issues of power, but also because of the resulting requirement to be in a constant state of openness and receptiveness.

Keeping one's head down, if it once was an option, no longer is. I am sure I am not alone in experiencing a certain stirring of recognition when John le Carré introduces us to Woodrow, the diplomat in his recent novel, *The Constant Gardener*:

> 'In his diplomatic career he [Woodrow] had been obliged to carry off any number of humiliating situations, and had learned by experience that the soundest course was to refuse to recognise that anything was amiss. He applied this lesson now . . . '.

Perhaps the world is becoming ever more embarrassed and embarrassing, as we struggle with the differences between us, the cultural *faux pas* and breaches of so-called political correctness. Perhaps it is taking us a little too long to recognise that the one certainty in all this change is not just change full stop, but the need to deal with and negotiate its cultural challenges. How, for example, would Woodrow rise to the findings of our recent perception research survey from Malawi, Zambia and Zimbabwe? Director of Central Africa, David Martin, calls for a better understanding of the aspirations, motivations, interests and perceptions of urban-based young people in the region – their hopes for the future, especially in terms of education, the views of their own society and their perceptions of the UK and other countries. Such research, designed to understand our customers and potential customers better, means that we can no longer assume that any of the traditional models of engagement will work in the countries in which we have a presence.

Hitherto in our 70-year history, we may have operated effectively to nurture relationships that benefit the UK while making contributions of value to large numbers of people around the world, without much recourse to the robust, globally inclusive and open internal dialogue recommended here. But times are changing, and changing rapidly. Received wisdom is coming under greater scrutiny. Increasingly, we have to ensure that suggestions emanating from our London or UK head office are wholly appropriate for our contexts and contacts. What important messages are being communicated: how and why are they being variously received? What really is the added value of a UK offering? What, if any, unique set of values can the UK claim as a deliverable? How do we share those aspects of UK culture that do not fit with perceptions and social norms elsewhere? And how best can we carry out our commitment to a mutuality of relationship inevitably determined by each specific situation, when there is a competing requirement for a 'global product'?

Nowadays, the British Council must pay close attention to all the potential lines of fracture in our societies; those caused, for example, by differences of age, social class, gender, race, sexuality, economic status, disability, religion, politics, or nationality. We must be alert to how difference is socially structured, and how this in turn, covertly and overtly, shapes our own attitudes, behaviour and interactions, whether in our work or in our internal management of diversity. For assuredly, in this process, we too will change. Cultural diversity cannot be an authentic or meaningful resource while our own role is purely reactive, whether out of a desire to please others, or to control them. Increasingly, we are coming to accept that cultural diversity pre-supposes a move from coexistence – with its static, essentialist notions of culture and the relations between cultures – to interrelation and mutual transformation.

If there is one more certainty for us in the British Council to ponder, it is that we are going to have to get together on this. No single formula will ensure that the multivalent process in which we are engaged is grounded in principles of human rights, respect, attentiveness to power and openness, leading to enrichment, progress and growth. No single space for decision-making in our multi-layered structure, at the level of the world, region, country, city, community, or organisation, will suffice to render us either critically self-reflective or coherent enough to survive the transformations ahead. Crucial too is the 'glue' that binds us together, so that we may be confident about what we are and why. Without a sense of common purpose, as well as a means of regulating and resolving inevitable conflicts, cultural diversity may indeed threaten our cohesion. In our organisation, as in society at large, people will hanker for the unity of an old world order that acquires a certain retrospective glow. Yet we know that there is no simple turning back. Diversity inevitably brings competing interests, realities and truths. We have started down a path in which the right to be equal and different has to be acknowledged, balanced and negotiated. If there is a return, it can be only to such 18th-century Enlightenment principles as the value of open debate. Ideas should be questioned: the good ones will catch on and the bad ones will be defeated. It isn't a perfect recipe, this intimate relationship between free speech and progress – it remains a strenuous balancing act.

Cultural homogeneity, however, is a contradiction in terms. Let us hope that the range of perspectives in this series will inspire many insights and questions for each one of us to take into our interactions, our work, and the great conversation of humankind.

The 'glue' that we seek will arise only from the gestation of value that Arjo Klamer locates in the 'dialogical process'. Imagine, as I did recently, while driving through one of our inner London boroughs, what impact a homogeneous world would have on our senses? Where would the broad stimulation, learning and pleasure as well as useful confusion and uncertainty – which make us feel truly 'alive' – come from? Of course, I must acknowledge my position of relative security in one of the world's more successful multicultural societies. Today, increasingly, my hope must be to live in a culturally diverse landscape that humanises, enriches and unifies all of us, not just some of us . . . in Mahatma Gandhi's words: 'I do not want my doors to be walled and my windows stuffed. I want the cultures of all lands to blow freely about my house. But I do not want to be blown off my feet by any.'

In the name of freedom

Jean-Michel Baer

Thanks to some brilliant British Enlightenment economists, it is widely accepted that the international division of labour and economic specialisation provide the world with a surplus of wealth.

The quantification of comparative advantage is actually the theoretical ground and *raison d'être* for all that has been done since the Second World War to foster the liberalisation of trade, via the General Agreement on Tariffs and Trade (GATT), the General Agreement on Trade in Services (GATS) and, more recently, the World Trade Organization (WTO).

Yet although the international debate over such liberalisation nominally covers the cultural sphere, no one has yet raised the question of what happens if such a theory is specifically applied to cultural goods or services. Can the global division of labour and economic specialisation be justified in practice in this sector?

Should the sole market mechanism be the 'invisible hand' enabling societies to reach a global 'cultural optimum'? Should states, regions or cities avoid distorting the free play of the market by enacting laws, applying rules, or by public subsidy, for example, to broadcasting, cinema, theatres, or opera? Imagine what absurdities would follow, were the principle of economic specialisation to prevail in this fashion. A country where theatre flourishes and cinema has declined would be inclined to hurl itself enthusiastically into specialising in, and further expanding, its theatrical sector, meanwhile renouncing cinema altogether! Absurd. However small the country, should it not aspire to develop the full range of its cultural creativity and products, whatever these might be?

It would seem that international free trade theories are hardly relevant in the field of culture, and that there is little theoretical justification, therefore, for including culture in the WTO negotiation round. This is why, at the beginning of the last session of the Uruguay Round, when the United States urged Europe to liberalise its audio-visual sector and apply to it the GATS disciplines – national treatment and market access commitments – the European Union (EU) replied that it would be keeping the right to regulate and support its audio-visual production and transmission. Such a commitment would have forced the EU and its member states to renounce all such preferential measures as subsidies, state aid or television quotas, now and for ever. How could this be acceptable?

Unanimity

This European response received unanimous backing from its member states. Under the Belgian presidency in October 1993, the famous Mons seminar of European culture ministers responsible for audio-visual matters drew up a framework of six guidelines. These sought to safeguard the freedom of individual governments in developing the policies they considered necessary to preserve the vitality of their cultures and their languages. This European position has been reaffirmed in the current Doha Round of the WTO. The EU has neither offered to liberalise its audio-visual sector, nor has it directed any request of this kind to its WTO partners.

As a policy approach, it cannot be described as protectionist. It simply belongs in a different category of international relations from trade relations. Nor has audio-visual trade between the United States and the European Union suffered at all from such a stance. Since the Marrakesh Agreements put an end to the Uruguay Round in 1994, the sales of American audio-visual programmes in Europe have grown by at least 10 to 15 per cent a year. American films still take about 70 per cent of the EU market, while the market share of European films in the United States remains strikingly weak, at 2 to 5 per cent. So, Europe is the more open market of the two: it certainly cannot be described as the most protectionist.

Several reasons might be advanced to explain why European governments have succeeded in reaching such a degree of unanimity on audio-visual matters. Let me mention three:

- A common vision of the importance of cinema and television for the cohesion of society. Each European country has invested in its own national public broadcasting service with a specific remit: pluralism in information, education, culture, moral and democratic well-being. Each country has drawn up public regulations for broadcasters for the general good of society: the protection of minors and human dignity, the regulation of advertising, and the promotion of national and European achievement.

- A common approach to the cinema ('the seventh art'), seen as belonging more to culture than to entertainment. Art and culture play a unique role, of course, in the representation of cultural and social values. If each country, together with its cultural heritage, is to be fully understood in a properly nuanced manner, it is necessary that each is in just as good a position to produce and distribute film, as it is to evolve its own literature or music. It is no accident that a wide range of mechanisms in every European state attempts to support the production and distribution of film.

- Last but not least, the 'acquis communautaire'. Thanks to the initiative shown by the Delors Commission during the years 1986–89, the European Community launched its audio-visual policy on two pillars: a regulatory pillar based on the Television Without Frontiers Directive; and such measures of financial support as the Media Programme, aimed at encouraging the transnational distribution of European films within the EU. The construction of the 'acquis' having been no mean feat, it has played an important role in the cohesion of the EU member states ever since, raising levels of awareness of the interdependence of national markets in Europe. For the success of Belgian or Danish film relies on the breadth of their distribution in Europe, outside Belgium and Denmark. Because UK cinemas are owned by American companies showing American movies, British films are shown more widely in the rest of Europe than in the UK itself.

Beyond diversity

Until recently, within the WTO, a large majority of states have shared the same viewpoint as Europe, and have decided not to commit themselves to the liberalisation of their audio-visual sector, as part of the WTO Services agreement. Among the strongest supporters of 'cultural exception', one might single out Australia, Canada, and South Africa for special mention. In 1998, Sheila Copps, Canadian Heritage Minister, took the initiative to set up the International Network on Cultural Policy – a network of culture ministers responsible for holding this line and promoting cultural diversity throughout the world. In 2003, this network undertook to ask UNESCO to draft an international convention that would provide these national cultural policies with more legal clout. The General Assembly of UNESCO agreed to the request. Drafting is under way and a draft proposal is expected in 2005. If everything goes well, globalisation in the field of culture will have furnished the means for nation states worldwide to preserve the diversity of their cultures.

Gradually, the notion of cultural diversity has caught on. For those who consider that democracy is more important than the market, and that a country must reserve its right to put into practice whatever is necessary for developing its culture or preserving its language, this is good news. Diversity is crucial – but in the present world, it is not sufficient.

The tragedy of 9/11 and the subsequent attack in Madrid certainly underline the need for closer links (information and common legal procedures) between the democracies. One lesson we have learnt from the 20th century is that without strength and determination democracy is soon threatened: we will never forget the exemplary courage of Great Britain in the Second World War. If we are to avoid a future clash of civilisations, it is our responsibility actively to promote the dialogue between cultures.

To this end, we must ensure equal flows of cultural exchange throughout the world and overall between the countries of the North and the South. What is required is a thorough overhaul of all the goals and mechanisms of our external cultural policies, to ensure that they reflect the urgent need for such intercultural dialogue. To have any hope of achieving this, European countries can and must co-operate more closely in the world at large. One example is the joint effort by German and French cultural services – supported by ARTE (the Franco-German cultural television channel) – to found a cultural centre in Ramallah together – a powerfully symbolic initiative showing that friendly co-operation is possible between yesterday's enemies.

Future initiatives
The EU initiatives I envisage under this heading could be twofold:

- A better integration of culture and the audio-visual industry into EU development policies (for example the Cotonou Agreement signed in June, 2000). This has two objectives: first, to help developing countries build the infrastructures for their cultural industries (we all recognise that these industries are not only a precondition of cultural creativity but also an important factor in economic growth and employment); second, to enable more equal cultural exchanges between the North and the South.
- An incentive for co-operation and joint initiative between the national cultural institutes or centres of the EU member states in third countries. These could set up common cultural platforms to showcase the variety and the unity of European cultures, as well as organising cultural dialogue and exchanges with the host country.

Such initiatives would soon become basic instruments of an effective cultural diversity policy. It is clear enough that if we want to foster cultural dialogue and exchanges, we have to help developing countries express their own creativity and extend a warmer welcome towards both that creativity and their cultural products.

Within this perspective, the UNESCO draft of the *International Convention on the Protection of the Diversity of Cultural Contents and Artistic Expressions* acquires tremendous importance as a source of encouragement. Its purpose will be to constitute a legal set of values, principles and standards providing a firm basis for the circulation of cultural ideas, cultural processes and products, throughout the world.

When it comes to universal values, it is crucial to affirm – as did the UNESCO *Declaration* of 2001 – that cultural pluralism and diversity are inseparable from the respect for human rights, fundamental freedom and human dignity: 'no one may invoke cultural diversity to infringe upon human rights nor limit their scope'.

What remains controversial in this future Convention is the clause on the capacity of every state, 'with due regard to its international obligations, to define its cultural policy and to implement it through the means it considers fit, whether by operational support or appropriate regulations'.

It is not so much the principle itself that raises objections: problems could arise from two directions:

- The difficulty of arriving at an exact definition of 'culture'. I need only refer you to Japan's attempts to protect its rice during the current Uruguay Round, by arguing that the cultivation of rice has cultural and aesthetic dimensions in Japanese tradition.
- Dealing with the so far hypothetical threat of closing down a market in culture altogether, that is, a country refusing to edit all but national writers; or only authorising the sales of national authors or the broadcasting of national films.

In these (and no doubt other cases) conflicts will occur. The question is: will the set of principles or rules be precise enough to avoid them? If not, what manner of international institution, and what kind of panel would have the competence to settle such conflicts?

If we admit the possibility that some measures of cultural policy could be contrary to the *Convention on the Protection of the Diversity of Cultural Contents and Artistic Expressions*, it is clear that a mechanism for the settlement of conflicts should be built into the framework of this legal instrument, to establish some cultural diversity criteria that can draw a clear line between the kind of national measure compatible with the principles of the Convention and those that are not.

So, if we take our second example, while it is obvious that a total exclusion of non-national authors from a national market is incompatible with the principles of cultural diversity and the rules of the Convention, the pros and cons of a partial exclusion, or a preference given to national cultural goods and services, are less clear. Everything hangs upon the precise level of this preference. Here, the experience of the European Union could be very useful. Any EU application of fundamental rights uses the principle of proportionality to assess whether or not a national measure is compatible with its Treaty. Both the EU Commission and the European Court of Justice monitor closely the proportionality of any measure taken to its stated objective. What this, crucially, ensures is that conflicts of a cultural nature will be examined in the light of cultural criteria – among them that of diversity – by a panel composed of experts in cultural matters.

Conclusion

This Convention should not be seen as an anti-WTO initiative. Its aim is to organise the development of cultural exchange in the world in such a way that real diversity is ensured, playing for culture the same role that the International Labour Organization plays in social policy, or International Environmental Conventions in the field of the environment.

In order to ensure harmonious relationships between the different international organisations, UNESCO has announced that the Convention working group on cultural diversity will work with the WTO, the World International Property Organization, and the United Nations Conference on Trade and Development on the precise terms of the agreement.

Many other questions remain to be addressed by UNESCO's experts, however:

- The framework of the rights and obligations of states in relation to international rights. If nation states remain free to define and implement a cultural policy preserving and promoting their own culture, should this policy not be compatible with the goals of the Convention? Take, for example, the development of balanced cultural exchanges in the world, that is, the access of cultural goods and services of developing countries to the northern market.
- The rights and obligations of states at national level as regards cultural diversity. We may observe in certain sectors a concentration of cultural supply which could be a threat to the cultural expression of minority groups and to cultural pluralism. In particular, to what extent does a state have the responsibility to maintain a balance between the interests of the 'majors' and independent companies?
- The working practices of the Convention. What kind of bodies should be instituted to enable the Convention to be implemented effectively, and what procedures adopted to settle any conflicts among members?

In the immediate aftermath of the Second World War, new international organisations were created with a view to reorganising relations between states and people. These were dedicated to the avoidance of war, and to the expression of solidarity – a common recognition that each country should benefit from world economic growth. Obviously, all these splendid goals have not been achieved. But the initiatives nevertheless constitute a remarkable step in what is indisputably the right direction.

Since then, other important concerns have appeared to dominate international decision-making. Two of them – the environment and culture – now demand a special effort, a new approach with redefined goals: sustainable development, balanced exchanges, and cultural diversity. Culture is at the heart of each collective of people: it represents the soul of a people, a group, a country. That is why we must treat culture with due respect and care. Whatever the economic interests at stake, a collectivity, a state respecting human rights, should remain free to express and develop its culture.

The economic nonsense of cultural diversity

Arjo Klamer

Can a people sell its cultural identity? Or buy it? Of course, they cannot. Cultural identity is not a commodity and therefore is not for sale or for purchase. But can a people lose its cultural identity by selling certain goods? Can a people gain in cultural identity by buying certain goods? Do the Japanese stand to lose part of their identity when trade in rice is freed? Do the Chinese gain by buying Western art? What if they were to purchase Rembrandt's *Night Watch* from the Dutch? What would that mean to them? And how would the deal affect Dutch society? In short, how much has trade to do with cultural identity?

The current preoccupation with cultural diversity appears to be motivated by a fear of the homogenisation allegedly brought about by the forces of international trade and globalisation. There is a sense that increasingly people all over the world listen to the same music, watch the same films and television series, wear similar clothes, eat the same food, and shop at the same stores. Local arts, and creative industries, folklore, crafts, and rituals appear to be losing out. Homogenisation makes for uniformity, so the reasoning continues, and that is at the expense of cultural diversity. And cultural diversity in itself is to be valued, more or less as biodiversity is (see Lalèyê and Throsby in this book). Such reasoning issues in a rallying cry to oppose the liberalisation of trade in cultural goods and comprehensive intellectual property rights, as such measures can only promote further homogenisation (read: Americanisation) and lessen cultural diversity.

Free traders cry 'nonsense' in response and point at the great cornucopia of diversity that free trade has unlocked. After all, thanks to free trade I can buy inexpensive kiwi fruits in my local store, have my pick of a vast variety of foodstuff, buy Italian designer shoes if I wished to do so, enjoy foreign films, listen to a wide array of music, admire Aboriginal art in a nearby museum, and mingle with people from all over the world. Free traders can be convincing these days. They have the aura of acting in the name of progress and change, while the culturalists, that is, those who insist on the preservation of cultural identities and values, seem conservative as they appear only to hold on to what has been. Free traders also have a less paternalistic and undemocratic air than culturalists, in insisting that it is their choice if French people want to watch American films rather than 'Frenchies', or Indonesians elect to watch American television rather than engage in local rituals. Who is to say, after all, that these people *should* prefer to hold on to traditional cultural practices and goods?

It is the fundamentalist stance on either side of this debate that I would like to tackle – and the either/or characteristic of the debate that I would like to undo. It cannot be the case that either you have to favour free trade in everything, including cultural goods, or have to desire the special protection of cultural goods; that you are either an economist (and in the main, a proponent of free trade) or a culturalist. The danger of being sucked into either position is indeed great because of the preoccupation with policy measures. Listening to the debates on intellectual property rights and free trade, you are made to believe that everything depends on what the countries of the World Trade Organization (WTO) will decide, and what measures they will put in place. It is as if a few politicians hold the fate of humanity in their hands; as if the combined actions of UNESCO, the European Union and so forth, will be able to turn around the way people live their lives and change their cultures. Society is a little too complicated for markets and governments to achieve this, I'd be willing to bet.

Within the *economic-cultural perspective* that I favour (see Klamer 1996, 2003, 2004), the cultural context figures large. Cultural and social values appear not as afterthoughts once the bulk of economic values have been accounted for, but as the kinds of values that human striving is all about. Economic values (think of income, wealth, profit, growth) are subsidiary. People earn money, make profit or strive for more growth in order to realise something social (family, friendship, community, nationality, identity and the like) or cultural (referring here to artistic and spiritual values, that is, values that are associated with something inspirational, sacred or transcendental).

I prefer to stress cultural values as distinct from social values, although I recognise the risk of confusion. The debate over cultural diversity is about social values, about identity and so forth, and not so much about the inspirational. To be sure, one's identity can be inspiring; and it would then have cultural value as I am using it here. But its primary function is social: it accords one recognition as a member of one particular group of people. When the arts are brought into the discussion, it is usually for the sake of their social values, and specifically what they mean for the shared identity of a particular group. Cultural (or inspirational) values are different. Aboriginal art, with its spiritual messages, may inspire quite a few Westerners, but for Aboriginal people it may well hold special social value (affirming their identity as a group apart in Australian society), as well as possessing economic value for as long as Westerners are willing to pay a good price for it.

From this economic-cultural perspective, the main question to arise in the debate on cultural diversity is: how are social values such as identity, tradition and a sense of community (having something in common with more or less well-identified other people) best realised? In which context do we human beings do best as social beings? Is it the market? Is it a well-organised state? Or must we look in a different direction? What circumstances best contain our sense of alienation and strengthen our sense of belonging? Allow me to pursue this line of questioning. Is it, for example, possible that we can have not only too much homogeneity, but also too much diversity? What if people feel excluded when 'others take over their streets and their jobs'? Witness the unexpectedly strong sentiments against so-called immigrants in much of Europe. Witness fanatical anti-Western feelings in much of the Islamic world. What is the diversity politicians and others interested in cultural diversity are really seeking? Is it diversity in the arts?

And what role, in fact, do the arts and other cultural goods play in all this? This last question is especially warranted in a context where sports and the news appear to signify a great deal more to our sense of identity than the arts. How important, actually, is a Damien Hirst for British identity, and how American are Madonna and Britney Spears? How Dutch is Van Gogh? Even if the Dutch are able to correctly pronounce Van Gogh's name, his works seem to signify most to others, to the Japanese in particular (who funded the expansion of the Van Gogh Museum in Amsterdam and who constitute its largest group of visitors, a number far exceeding the few Dutch who take the trouble to visit the museum).

My claim is that neither the market nor a government (national or international) is best placed to inculcate important social and cultural values. Insofar as these modernist institutions have a role to play, it is a subsidiary one at best. Art, too, has a minor, if exquisite, role. Dominant social and cultural values come about outside and beyond the spheres of the market, the government or the arts. Let me explain.

The cynic versus the romantic

The economist in me obliges me to pose awkward questions and define tough choices. Economics, when it comes down to it, is about the trade-offs we all have to make. Resources are scarce. Everything we do has costs. Everything. Time is money: art costs money. There are no free lunches. I have learned enough to know how appropriate the input of economists can be – especially when those romantics prevail who, in Oscar Wilde's memorable characterisation, know the value of everything but the price of nothing. Let romantics rule the roost, and the world turns wild. The sobering input of economists is needed from time to time to counterbalance the romantic impulse. When one spouse walks in to announce that he, or she, has decided to pursue the meaning in life, and dedicate that life to the arts, or religion, giving up the day job that sustains the family, the other may well wish to point out the costs of this sudden outburst of the romantic spirit: not only in lost income – after all, the house may need to be sold and the kids can forget about private education. Doing art has a price; sustaining a world conducive to the arts is costly. This message needs to be heard from time to time.

Yet I am also uncomfortable with the economic stance. The reason is its inevitable association with Oscar Wilde's cynic: he who knows the price of everything and the value of nothing. Unfortunately, my profession provides plenty of fuel for such a suspicion, with its unfettered aspiration to attach price labels to everything existing and conceptualise economic behaviour as if it were a matter of mere calculation. Beauty, ideals, dreams and everything else that the romantic values are simply givens in the systems that economists develop. Exciting indeed if you happen to be one of those people who like to play with numbers and formulae; but it tends to repel everyone else.

In hindsight: changing notions of value

To counter the cynic, it helps to revisit the past of economics. There we discover that a single-minded focus on numbers is a relatively recent phenomenon within the discipline. As a matter of fact, economics began its days as a moral discourse, with an overriding interest in the concept of value. Aristotle, to name one of the very first thinkers who paid attention to economic matters of concern, saw value as residing in the essence or core nature of the thing being valued. In the Middle Ages, Catholic thinkers took after him, with the difference that they more explicitly recognised God's handiwork in the value of things. It followed that people had to respect God's will, not only in the church but also in the market place, by trading according to His value, or, as it was called, the just price. Inspired by the Scottish Enlightenment, Adam Smith took matters out of God's hands and put them into the hands of the working man. Thanks to his intervention, the labour that went into the production of a commodity was subsequently viewed as the value-determining factor. The idea would spark Marx's revolutionary project of worker-empowerment. Only at the end of the 19th century, when economists began to veer away from speculation about the value of things, turning instead to the concept of the mechanical hands of the marketplace, did the moral connotations of the concept of value fade into the background of the economic discipline. Ever since, the notion of value has been appropriated by moral philosophers and a handful of politicians, here or there.

It is time to retrieve something of the discipline's moral antecedents. Such thinking is what lies behind the aforementioned cultural economic perspective, in which appreciation of culture brings with it respect for the economic aspects of cultural trade: the romantic travels hand in hand with the cynic. The insight that results might well suggest that under certain conditions the economic options are perfectly reasonable – such as selling the *Night Watch* and holding on to the day job as opposed to pursuing a romantic impulse; yet under other circumstances, holding on to the *Night Watch* and forsaking the benefits of a job for a life dedicated to culture, might make perfect sense as well.

The argument that follows rejects any form of fundamentalism in the discussion on the free trade in cultural goods. Economics is not sacred: but neither is culture nor cultural identity. Let us agree from the outset that the issue is negotiable. Only negotiations can determine where we come down on the issue of cultural protection. The quality of these negotiations will determine whether we will be pleased with the outcome. The only feasible opening stance to adopt towards the treatment of cultural trade in general is one of ambivalence.

Economists and free trade
In its advocacy of free trade my profession distinguishes itself. You might even say that it defines the discipline. Once upon a time, protection was perceived as the pathway to riches. The mercantilists preached a doctrine of strength: colonise richly endowed foreign territories or do whatever it takes to accumulate wealth at home, including thwarting other trade. The doctrine continues to be popular, the arguments of economists notwithstanding. Beginning with David Hume and Adam Smith, they have claimed that generally nations do better with free trade. David Ricardo, another well-known classical economist, even entered the British Parliament to make his case against the protectionist Corn Laws. The argument is pretty simple but can be developed in the form of sophisticated mathematical models. It is that if people are left to their own devices, including in their exchange with foreigners, society as a whole will be better off. It is a matter of efficiency. That's why economists in general love the WTO and what it stands for. Any step taking us closer to liberalisation is good. It is a question of the open hand versus the tight fist. The argument of Adam Smith is that of the open hand: laissez-faire. Let the people go! Protectionists are tight-fisted. They want to hold on to what is.

The arguments of tight-fisted protectionists have little chance of making headway against the open-handed recommendations of Adam Smith and his fellow free-marketeers. Usually they are intended to protect the interests of a small group in society – the farmers, say, or the textile workers, or those working in the film industry. Free trade could hurt those groups who can't compete with cheap foreign agricultural produce, textiles, or films. 'That's not fair!', it is argued, and so the government has to protect them.

In virtually all known cases, the cure will only make matters worse. Yes, those groups that were initially hurt, benefit, but many more are negatively affected. Think of the consumers. They have to pay the price for protection: they pay more for agricultural products, clothes, and films. And that is not fair either. One $30,000 job saved in the textile industry would cost society $200,000. So it would be cheaper just to hand the guy $40,000 with an additional $10,000 by way of compensation for the emotional pain suffered. The costs of protecting the jobs of a few are high. The question to you and me is: are the jobs saved worth those extra costs? We may decide that they are. And then, we may want the general interest to prevail.

Trusting open-handed policy has also proved difficult. It seems to go against nature. Policy-makers want to be in control, and voters like to see their politicians make a fist when times get tough. Businesses generally favour the open-hand approach, as they want to be left alone in their pursuit of profit; yet they, too, are well-known for not being above insisting on tight-fisted policy when it comes to foreign trade. When the American steel industry got into trouble due to foreign competition at the end of the 1970s, its bosses – erstwhile champions of open-handed capitalism – trooped off shamelessly enough to Washington to ask the US government to use its fist against 'unfair' foreign competition. As a consequence, American jobs were saved, but American consumers paid the price.

We economists call this behaviour 'rent-seeking'. It is the pursuit of profit by political means, that is, by lobbying for measures that protect profits. Rent-seeking is all around us. Currently, we are seeing cultural industries actively pursuing this strategy with the European film industry leading the way. European consumers flock to American films, so European film producers want to see some fists waved by their governments, lest they lose their income. If you can't beat them in the market, beat them in politics: that's what the game is about. At least, so it seems from the economics perspective.

For sure, protectionists will argue, without a tight-fisted policy on the part of European governments we can all wave the European film industry goodbye. A pretty convincing argument points a further finger at the protectionist policies of the US government towards its own film industry, which paved the way for the emergence of its monopoly in foreign distribution. The economists' answer is that a tight-fisted policy tends to be wasteful, only stimulating unproductive rent-seeking activities. When governments demonstrate eagerness to protect, business managers will dedicate massive resources to lobbying and other types of political activity, at the expense of other more productive efforts.

This does not exhaust the case for the tight-fisted approach. One strong argument in its favour is the 'infant-industry phenomenon'. Budding industries, it is argued, such as the European film industry, are vulnerable and therefore need protection to flower. Supporting evidence is provided by modern Japan and South Korea, where protection of infant industries seems to have led to mature and powerful agglomerations. Unfortunately, there is plenty of counter-evidence. In Ghana and Argentina, for example, protected infant industries have continued to produce second-rate and overpriced products. Even in Korea and Japan the positive effects are dubious as consumers paid a heavy price for the protectionist policies, and some of the agglomerations are still faltering.

The economics of cultural trade
Turn now to the case of artistic and cultural goods and activities. In a useful survey, the economists Frey and Pommerehne (1993) have investigated the economic justifications for restrictions in the international trade in cultural artifacts. Many countries strictly regulate the export, but not the import, of art 'treasures', including paintings. As may be expected of economists, Frey and Pommerehne do not think that the justifications for such policies withstand scrutiny from the economic perspective. As a matter of fact, the economic evidence points to the advantages of liberalisation of cultural trade.

One economic argument in favour of free trade is simply that the free traders will be better off. Take the fact that the rates of return on art investments are lower than the rates on financial investments; a country could simply increase its income by selling its paintings, investing the revenues, and buying back the paintings later. Furthermore, liberalisation of trade could enhance prospects for the consumers of culture, since it would make available work that is never exhibited, due to the space constraints of its current owner. Allowing the Getty Museum or the Japanese to buy work that is now held in storage by the Prado would at least give the public a chance to see it, even if it is in Los Angeles or Kobe. And the Prado would have funds that are badly needed for its upkeep.

The economic arguments are also stacked in favour of the liberalisation of the European market for films. In the context of these trade negotiations, the European film industry was successful in creating an exception in the final draft with the argument that the cultural integrity of Europe was at stake. Apparently, the idea is that the EU market requires protection against the domination of the American film industry, lest the European Union is gradually Americanised. This idea prevailed: cultural integrity still has a sacred aura – anyone touching it risks being labelled a cultural barbarian. Reality, however, is sobering. A long history of protectionist measures (such as quotas for American productions on television) and subsidies, has not prevented a dramatic deterioration in the relative position of the European film industry. Most telling are the numbers of visitors: during the 1980s, attendance at European cinemas dropped by 350 million visitors from 900 to 550 million, but virtually the entire drop is accounted for by the loss in audience for European films, interest for American films remaining more or less constant during this period.[1] On the surface, increased protection in this case weakened the ability to produce movies for mass consumption. A similar saga can be told about the European television industry which has an increasing struggle to produce programmes that can compete with the American supply.

From the economists' point of view, reasons for the failure of protectionist programmes are clear enough. One reason has to do with incentives. As noted above, a regime of subsidies and restrictions stimulate unproductive rent-seeking activities, with producers 'working the corridors of power' to secure funds for their pet projects rather than 'working the market'. Furthermore, the preferences of those who control the subsidy channels are decisive rather than those who are the ultimate 'consumers' of the cultural goods. Consequently, the producers of such goods are encouraged to play to the wrong crowd.

With all these negative effects in mind economists favour the stimulation that the open-handed approach provides. In their world, artists and film producers compete for attention in a worldwide market, unimpeded by all kinds of artificial barriers. No matter what you think of economists – and they can indeed be quite tedious – their arguments need to be taken seriously.

The chancy benefits of concentration

You may by now be drawing the conclusion that this is an unmitigated plea for free trade and the open-handed policy. If so, you've been too hasty. I wanted only to give you a strong taste of the persuasiveness of the economic perspective on the issue of free trade. We could now proceed to the non-economic arguments that can be claimed on behalf of tight-fisted policies. Think of the usual, culturalist, claims of the importance of culture for the overall health of any community, the relevance of cultural autonomy for its identity, the educative value of culture, and the importance of equal, or relatively inexpensive, access to cultural products. But there are also economic arguments that protectionists could use. In other words, the French have good economic reasons to hold out for the exception of certain cultural goods. Consider two of those reasons: one, an extension of the externality argument; the other concerning the culture of economics.

The externality argument is closely related to the infant-industry argument. It has to do with what it takes to generate a productive and creative environment. It was the well-known economist Paul Krugman who first pointed out the geographical factor in economic growth (1994). He noticed that many successful industries tend to be concentrated in a relatively small region, often with the active support of local and central governments, in the form of airports, roads, and tax advantages. His famous example is the seemingly insurmountable advantage in the construction of aeroplanes built up throughout this century within the region around Seattle. All the big aeroplane manufacturers happen to be located in that wet part of north-west USA. And it all began by chance. One company chose the site for some reason or another, and happened to do well. In the process an infrastructure developed in support of this industry, so when other companies sought a location in which to set up shop, the Seattle region stood out. There they would be guaranteed the presence of critical suppliers, understanding government bureaucracies and, most importantly, a pool of skilled workers.

Examples of similar concentrations abound. Think of Hollywood. The film industry started here by chance when it needed sufficient sunlight, and now, firmly established, continues to attract anyone who wants to do something in the movies. In the Netherlands, Hilversum has become a centre for producers of music and television programmes only because that is where the radio and television stations happen to be established. The Silicon Valley developed, again by chance, as a centre for the computer industry.

Michael Porter, the current management guru, underscores Krugman's externality argument (Porter, 1990). His emphasis is on the synergy that is generated when people work closely together. That's why shoemakers, diamond cutters, artists, and professionals of all kinds like to work in close proximity. Even though they are in competition, they need each other. By clustering in a small area, they stimulate their suppliers to set up shop nearby, so that they can easily exchange information, draw on the same pool of experienced workers, and have the opportunity to chat. Only a few thrive in isolation. Competition in proximity tends to stimulate creativity. That is why political and scientific interest in cultural clusters has been surging during the last few years.

However, although Krugman and Porter appear to provide strong arguments for the protection of the cultural industries of, say, Europe against competition from the USA, and the active support of governments for the growth of cultural clusters, it is dubious whether such policy measures in the name of their theories will be effective. To be sure, politicians could pick a region, bring all film-makers together, provide them with the best infrastructure imaginable, including the proper educational institutions, and get something like a new Hollywood going – just as the Europeans launched their Airbus project to tackle the supremacy of the Seattle area. Maybe politicians can indeed make some difference by motivating certain groups of professionals to get together by providing the necessary infrastructure and developing the proper educational institutions. But there are problems. A major one is that politicians all over the place are trying this strategy, and setting up centres of excellence and industry parks, and that far from everyone is succeeding. As Krugman had already noted, luck plays a role, too. Being too tight-fisted about this may not work. The free hand should be given a chance as well. That requires a sensitivity that is usually too much for our pragmatic politicians. Yet, it is the only constructive way. Support, and the creation of favourable conditions: that is what the policy should be about. But apart from these tight-fisted measures, rely on the policy of the open hand. That would be my advice.

The culture of economics
The other reason to suspect the economists' perspective was lurking in our brief visit to the past of economics. If you recall, this led us to the concept of 'value' and the moral meanings that economists originally

attached to it. Transfer such concerns to the current context and we might be moved to consider the values inherent in free trade. Once left free to their own devices people have to give form to their interactions. According to the picture that economists sketch, they do so in the context of markets. It makes for a rosy picture in this book of economics – the market price as the magic instrument that makes everything work and guarantees the greatest happiness for all. Yet this free market world can be ugly, too. The market, as well as being magical, is harsh; it causes anxiety and trauma. And it forces us into anonymous and mechanical relationships, one with another. Markets seem to turn everything and everybody into a thing.

Markets are about exchanges in equivalence. When the Chinese pay the Dutch $200 million for the *Night Watch*, one thing is exchanged for the other. The money and the painting change hands, a handshake follows – maybe – and that's that. The deal is done. It works fine in many cases. When we transact business in the supermarket, for example, I hand over $20 and get a bag of groceries in exchange. That's it.

But that is not how it always works. Fortunately. In many, if not most, transactions with fellow human beings the principle of reciprocity prevails. We exchange, but the when, how, and what of the *quid pro quo* remains undetermined. Friends do me a favour and I will return the favour if I'm a good friend. The when, how, and what will have to be determined later. My parents took care of me when I was young. I will honour the memory of my father in exchange, and be nice to my mother and offer care when she needs it. It is a question of reciprocity. We do it all the time. And we do it for good reason. For that is how we bring about relationship. When reciprocity reigns, the deal is never done – as in a pure market transaction. Reciprocity brings about indebtedness and, more positively, a bonding. It gives a relationship its moral character.

Cultural goods are different because they do not suffer the phase of the market, the *quid pro quo* deal, lightly. Goods like friendship, cultural identity, religion, truth, and love are highly valuable socially and culturally – but they are not for sale or purchase. Their values cannot be expressed in price and, more importantly, do not lend themselves to an exchange in equivalences. The same applies to cultural goods, or at least certain dimensions of them. Because of the Dutch identification with Rembrandt's *Night Watch*, selling it is inconceivable. Pricing such a painting is as meaningless, and offensive, as it would be to price a friendship, or a child. Time is involved, and bonding, too. Some goods need time. We have invested in them and once they begin to bear fruit – in the form of feelings of pride, love, awe even – giving them up in a done deal is inconceivable; selling a friendship or a treasure would be like the betrayal of all we stand for. Uncertainty is a factor as well. We can never be sure of the value of those special goods. How much is your child worth to you? How much do you want me to sell your wedding ring for? Is the *Night Watch* worth a $100 million, or $1 billion? When we have to exchange what is most precious to us, we may prefer to do so in a deal where reciprocity is also present. So the Dutch might lend out the *Night Watch* – although that is inconceivable right now even while the Rijksmuseum is being renovated – but only if the Chinese were to return the favour somehow, in a big way, at some other time. In that way we may find value in the deal itself, that is, in the quality of the reciprocal exchange.

How values come about

Culture is fragile – although maybe not defenceless as the Dutch painter–poet Lucebert once famously declared everything of value to be. But while some of us are convinced of the value of experimental theatre, literature, art films, and old paintings, others care less. The value of culture, therefore, is contestable. Could that be why we tend to be careful with it – as if culture is something as sacred as religion once was? Whatever the reason, it might be a good argument for paying some kind of cultural activities special attention. This is why

French resistance against the treatment of cultural goods as just another product (or service) is a welcome political move. It guarantees a passionate discussion in which participants will be forced to re-evaluate the value of their cultural goods.

Imagine Chinese demand is such that they try to buy the *Night Watch* for a hefty sum. The very proposal would compel the Dutch to re-evaluate the value of this painting, and to reassess the importance of their cultural heritage. In the ensuing discussions, the Dutch, as well as the Chinese, would quickly discover everything that Rembrandt means to them, how some Dutch probably care a great deal and others care less, and what it takes to convince those in doubt. In the process, the Dutch will get entangled in evaluations of their heritage, and will have to argue about their identity and their future. This is, incidentally, more or less what has already happened once, in the 19th century. Then, public interest in Rembrandt was small. In 1828 the Dutch government had bought a single Rembrandt (*The Anatomy Lesson of Professor Tulp*) and that was it.[2] In 1880, only ten Rembrandts were in public hands. Foreign demand changed the situation. Thanks to the eager interest in Rembrandts, above all on the part of Americans, the Dutch were compelled to re-evaluate their own stock of Rembrandts. As a result of this re-evaluation, the government undertook actions to prevent the exports of Rembrandts, and Rembrandt became a recognised national treasure.

It follows that the extent to which the Dutch value their Rembrandt, together with all the other signs of Dutchness like Volendam and the windmills, is determined in and through processes of negotiation. Outside pressure can be instrumental in getting these negotiations started. It is the open-handed approach that keeps the people on edge, leading them to realise what they have and want to have – or better still, what they are and want to be. It is protectionist measures that generate discussion and a process of evaluation and revaluation. What counts is that people are in conversation. Only in the dialogical process can we find out the values of all that we have or all that we want to be. And this dialogue takes place mainly outside the spheres of the market and the government, in the third sphere, also called 'civil society'.

Activities with borders
When the focus is on markets and governments controlling markets, it is easy to overlook the fact that most human activities, most interactions, take place outside their spheres of influence (Klamer and Zuidhof, 1999). People tend to do most in the context of families, groups, clubs, societies, nations and unions in order to construct and acknowledge the values that they have in common, values like a common heritage, an identity, a welfare system, heroes, traditions and rituals. They talk, share, care, love, but also struggle, argue with and oppress other people in the social contexts of civil society – without the intervention of market mechanisms or bureaucratic rules. That is how cultures come about – in the social sense, that is. People tend to go about in groups and will do things in order to distinguish themselves from other groups. They will keep outsiders out, cherish certain goods as typically theirs, consider some goods as sacred just to maintain a sense of 'us'.

Note the efforts of the European Union to foster a sense of 'we, Europeans'. The realisation is dawning that economic measures do not suffice to generate such a sense. The euro does not necessarily unite the culturally diverse groups that make up Euroland. That is why some argue for the need for a cultural policy. If only European artists would work more closely together, or if only creative industries developed on a European scale, maybe a European 'we' would come about. European politicians would like nothing better than that Europeans considered themselves distinct from Chinese people, Americans, Indians and Russians, and would feel European in addition to feeling British or Dutch. But would this automatically follow, were they to be treated to more Damien Hirst and watch more French films? I doubt it.

In their cultural policies, European politicians have realised the need for borders. Europe has to be a bordered entity in order to generate social values like a European identity. Claims that its cultural diversity makes the European Union distinct begin to sound empty as Europeans continue to search for the something in common they need to feel just that, European. Cultural diversity has a meaning only when people associate themselves foremost with one, rather than another culture.

My point is that most cultural activity takes place more or less spontaneously outside the sphere of the market and the government. It happens when people associate, when they form groups. Such groups will limit their interactions with outsiders. Just as friends will prefer to talk with each other rather than with strangers, and family members tend to be preoccupied with other members, nationals prefer to conduct political and business affairs among themselves rather than with different nationals. Politicians may want to stimulate this, but usually it is not necessary. British sports fans care almost exclusively about the achievements of British sportsmen and women – and need no politician to tell them to do so. Italians continue to eat Italian without much of a policy to support this cultural practice. There is no call to ban Thai people or MacDonalds from opening restaurants in Rome. Maybe political measures can stimulate or discourage such identifications, but they cannot impose, manage, control or eradicate them. For example, exposure to other cultures, the encounter with the other, may actually strengthen the identification with one's own culture. That may be one reason why people travel and seek the encounter with artifacts of other cultures.

The question remains: can cultural practices be shielded from foreign influence by means of a tight-fisted approach? When they yield under the pressure of foreign practices and goods, they may be insufficiently strong to be sustainable anyway. In some cases foreign interests – tourists, say – may bring about a revival of local cultures. But in the end, cultural diversity thrives only when inspired by the typical human inclination to form groups that are distinct from others.

Endnotes

[1] For this and further information, see the report by the think tank, 1994.

[2] See Cees Bruyn, 1995.

Bibliography

Bruyn, Cees, Rembrandt, 1995, 'Verzamelaars en Internationaal Cultuurbezit'.
In J. Heilbron, W. de Nooy, W Tichelaar (eds). *Waarin een Klein Land.*
Nederlandse Cultuur in Internationaal Verband. Amsterdam: Prometheus.

European Commission, 1994, *Report by the Think-Tank on the Audiovisual*
Policy in the European Union. Luxemburg.

Klamer, Arjo (ed.), 1996, *The Value of Culture*.
Amsterdam: Amsterdam University Press.

Klamer, Arjo, 2003, 'A Pragmatic View on Values in Economics',
Journal of Economic Methodology, vol. 10, no.2, pp. 191–212.

Klamer, Arjo, 2004. 'Cultural Goods are good for more than their economic
value'. In V. Rao and M. Walton (eds). *Culture and Public Action*. Stanford
California: Stanford University Press, pp. 138–62.

Klamer, Arjo and PW Zuidhof, 1999, 'The Values of Cultural Heritage: Merging
Economic and Cultural Appraisal'. In M. de la Torre and R. Mason (eds),
Economics and Heritage Conversation, Los Angeles: The Getty Conservation
Institute, pp. 23–61.

Krugman, Paul, 1994, *Peddlers of Prosperity*, New York: Basic Books.

Pommerehne, Werner, and Bruno S. Frey, 1993, 'Justifications for Art Trade
Restrictions: The Economic Perspective'. *Etudes en Droit de l'Art*, no. 3, pp. 89–114.

Porter, Michael, 1990, *The Competitive Advantage of Nations*, New York:
Free Press.

Lalèyê, Issiaka-P. Latoundji, 2004, in this volume.

Throsby, David, 2004, in this volume.

Sweetness and light? Cultural diversity in the contemporary global economy
David Throsby

'[Culture] seeks . . . to make all men live in an atmosphere of sweetness and light, where they may use ideas, as it uses them itself, freely – nourished and not bound by them.'
Matthew Arnold, *Culture and Anarchy,* 1869

What is cultural diversity?
An American medical aid worker in a remote village in El Salvador dispenses antibiotics to a sick child. In a schoolroom in Melbourne a teacher gives a lesson in Aboriginal history to students whose families have migrated to Australia from Britain, Italy, Greece, Lebanon, Vietnam and China. A social worker in München counsels a Turkish woman on problems she is encountering in her workplace. A theatre director in Birmingham rehearses actors from various ethnic backgrounds in a play about cultural interaction in suburban England. For all these workers, cultural diversity is a matter of everyday life, a daily reality in the pursuit of their professional duties. In each case the cultural difference between themselves and the people they are dealing with simply adds a further dimension to the complexities of their task. For some of them cultural diversity is a source of tension requiring careful handling to avoid misunderstanding and conflict; for others it is a joyful recognition of the richness and multiplicity of human life.

Similarly in communities themselves. Where, for example, racial differences are apparent, cultural diversity can mean different things to different people. It can be a source of hostility between social groups, even leading to vilification and violence. Alternatively, it can be an avenue to greater intercultural dialogue, understanding and creativity.

But the phenomenon of cultural diversity transcends these individual experiences, projecting itself onto the very nature of the societies in which we live, and raising critical questions about forms of social and political organisation and governance. In ethically diverse countries – and that means the great majority of countries in the modern world – such questions include: How much, and what sort of, diversity is desirable? Is cultural pluralism possible within a democratic state? Does cultural differentiation increase or diminish within society over time? How is cultural diversity affected by the spread of globalisation? Is it possible to encourage greater recognition of diversity without also increasing social and political instability?

If we take an even wider view, and move from the perspective of the community, the region, or the nation state, to that of the whole of humankind, we can embrace a global vision for cultural diversity. Such a vision has been spelt out recently by the United Nations Educational, Scientific and Cultural Organisation (UNESCO) in its *Universal Declaration on Cultural Diversity*, a document unanimously adopted by the UNESCO General Conference at a meeting held shortly after 9/11. The *Declaration* is based on the premise that intercultural dialogue is the best guarantee of peace. It rejects the proposition that the 'clash of civilisations' is an inevitable condition of the contemporary world.

What sort of cultural diversity did the UNESCO member states endorse? The 12 articles of the *Declaration* encompass identity, human rights, creativity and international solidarity. Together they comprise a comprehensive account of how far the notion of cultural diversity can be taken to extend in contemporary international discourse. According to this document, cultural diversity can be defined in the following terms. First, diversity is seen as being embodied in the 'uniqueness and plurality' of the identities of various societies and groups – a common heritage of humankind. Since culture itself is intrinsic to the realisation of human aspirations, it is argued that cultural diversity will be an important factor in promoting economic, social and cultural development in both industrialised and developing countries. Second, the *Declaration* asserts that promotion of cultural diversity can take place only in accordance with respect for fundamental human rights. No one should invoke cultural diversity in order to defend, for example, 'traditional' cultural practices that deny basic rights and freedoms, such as those of women or of minorities.

A third aspect of cultural diversity identified in the *Declaration* is the recognition it accords the distinctive nature of cultural goods and services such as films, artworks, television programmes, music recordings, and so forth. Apart from being commercial commodities, these goods have an important role to play as purveyors of cultural messages. Since cultural goods and services arise from human creativity, it follows that cultural diversity will be enhanced in conditions conducive to creative activity and to the production and distribution of a wide range of cultural products. Finally, the UNESCO member states declared that international co-operation and dialogue involving public institutions, the private sector and civil society will be required to enable the benefits arising from cultural diversity to have effect worldwide.

Why is cultural diversity valued?
While the *Universal Declaration* is concerned with setting the broader context, we can define cultural diversity more succinctly as the manifold ways in which humans express themselves in artistic and cultural terms. Over recent years, this diversity has been compared increasingly with the vast differentiation observable in nature, that is, biodiversity. As scientists have been able to articulate

the value of biodiversity more and more clearly, it has proved possible to carry the parallel forward and to point to similar ways in which the value of cultural diversity can be expressed. Four sources of value emerge from this exercise.

To begin with, we know that biodiversity is valued for its own sake; people appreciate the infinite variety of plant and animal life on the planet, just because it is there. By the same token it can be argued that the variety of cultural expressions is seen as important *per se*, and valued as a part of the 'human mosaic'. This source of value, in economic terms, is a public good deriving from the 'existence value' of the diversity in question – people gain benefit simply from the knowledge that both biodiversity and cultural diversity exist.

The second source of value lies in the interconnectedness of the cultural world, which resembles that found in nature. No species exists in isolation; neither do cultures. If species are isolated from each other, they stagnate and die; so do cultures. Thus the webs of relationships in both biological and cultural spheres are valued. If these are damaged, diversity is diminished.

Furthermore, these natural and cultural 'ecosystems' are necessary to support economic activity. Over the past decade or so there has been a growing awareness of the interdependence between the economy and the air, land and water systems that make up the natural environment. Recently, we have begun to understand more clearly that cultural ecosystems – the invisible networks and relationships that hold cultures together and give meaning to people's lives – are just as important in underpinning the economic processes of production, consumption and exchange. People are not automatons working in a vacuum, and they cannot be economically productive if their cultural infrastructure breaks down.

Finally, biodiversity is valued because some species *may* have economic value as yet unrecognised. Society should therefore be concerned by any loss of species diversity because this could incur economic costs or forgone opportunities in the future. A similar proposition can be made in the cultural sphere: certain cultural manifestations may have both economic and cultural value that is not yet evident. Hence cultural diversity is valuable because it keeps options open for the future. Moreover, preservation of those options requires adoption of the so-called precautionary principle, whereby extreme caution must be exercised in making decisions that could result in the permanent loss of some item of cultural capital – a ritual, a language, or a historic building, for example.

The current debate

The *Universal Declaration on Cultural Diversity* paints a glowing picture of an idealised world, one where people of all races, social classes and stages of economic development live together in mutual harmony, expressing their own cultural identity while engaging in dialogue and fruitful exchanges with people from other cultural backgrounds.

But the real world at the start of the third millennium seems a long way from such a vision. The Cold War may be over, but new sources of instability have emerged and the media remind us daily of the violence and intolerance that affect people's lives in so many parts of the world. Persistent economic inequalities go some way towards explaining this global discord, but conflict over cultural differences is clearly a significant factor as well. In these circumstances the *Universal Declaration*, for all its good intentions, could easily be dismissed as empty rhetoric.

Delegates sitting around the UNESCO conference table in Paris in November 2001 were mindful of this danger. They realised that something more than just a declaration would be needed if the profile of culture in national and international affairs were to be raised, and the positive benefits flowing from cultural diversity maximised. They recognised that an international treaty would be required, an instrument that would not only identify the *rights* of countries to take action in the cultural sphere, but also spell out their *obligations* to protect and enhance the world's cultural diversity. To be effective, the treaty would have to be established and implemented through the United Nations system and carry with it all the authority that world body could muster.

In retrospect, looking beneath the surface, we can see that the impetus towards a UN Convention on Cultural Diversity has come particularly from three interrelated sources: continuing problems with cultural goods and services in international trade; the perceived effects of globalisation on the world's cultures; and North/South imbalances in access to cultural resources and in capacities to foster sustainable cultural development.

Culture and trade

Ever since the ratification of the General Agreement on Tariffs and Trade (GATT) in the immediate post-war years, cultural goods and services – particularly films, television programmes and other audio-visual products – have been an irritant, thwarting the achievement of total trade liberalisation. The notion of a 'cultural exception' has been introduced as a means of excluding cultural products from the legal framework governing international trade. Debate about this and other possible measures to deal with culture within the successors to the GATT – the World Trade Organization (WTO) and the General Agreement on Trade in Services (GATS) – has been vigorously engaged between countries favouring liberalisation, principally the United States, and those seeking a mechanism for cultural protection, including, particularly, Canada and France.

In the specific context of cultural diversity, the argument for liberalisation goes beyond simply the standard economic rationale for free trade based on the principles of comparative advantage and consumer sovereignty. It suggests that cultural diversity is actually enhanced rather than diminished by free competition in the cultural field. By making an ever wider array of cultural products available to consumers, the free market allows consumers greater diversity in the ranges of choices available to them. Further, it is suggested that sheltering domestic production of, say, films and television programmes from foreign competition, will breed cultural complacency and lack of dynamism in these industries. The presence of imported product, on the other hand, will stimulate local producers to strive for greater distinctiveness in their output.

On the other side of the fence, the call for protection also relies on both economic and cultural arguments. The familiar economic grounds used to justify protection of domestic industries of whatever sort – market failures, infant-industry arguments, and so on – can be invoked in the case of cultural goods. If American films displace French ones in Parisian cinemas, the supposedly positive external benefits from the latter will be diminished. Moreover, the substantial scale economies enjoyed by the Hollywood producers mean they can sell their products into French markets at a fraction of the cost of producing films in France, denying the domestic industry the chance to grow and ultimately reap those same scale economies for itself. Cultural arguments for protection, by contrast, rely on non-economic considerations concerning the importance of domestically produced cultural goods and services in conveying symbolic messages about local, regional and national cultures. Excessive competition from cultural imports, it is argued, will result in a lessening of cultural diversity, since national industries will decline, or will respond in imitative ways that encourage a homogenisation of production.

Where is the truth in these contrasting positions? The answer, predictably, lies somewhere in between. Evidence can be assembled to support both sides; in some circumstances liberalisation certainly promotes diversity, but at the same time experience in other situations suggests just the opposite. So it has to be accepted that different situations will require different policy responses at the national level, if the aim is to promote cultural diversity through regulation or otherwise of trade in cultural goods. In other words, one size will not fit all.

One particular problem in dealing with culture in the international trade arena has been the dominance of the standard neo-liberal economic paradigm in setting the rules of the game. There is no doubt that once it is admitted that cultural considerations are important in their own right in defining and determining national objectives, the cultural content of creative goods does endow them with a significance or value that is rather different from their economic or commercial value. I have argued that once this proposition is accepted, it becomes more appropriate to talk about cultural *recognition* than about cultural *exception* when referring to trade in cultural goods. Such a recognition would have the effect of elevating the objectives of cultural policy to equal status with those of economic policy on the national and international agenda.

What follows from acknowledging the so-called 'specificity' of cultural goods and services in the international trading system is that ways need to be devised to put it into effect. A number of mechanisms have been discussed for adapting existing trade rules to allow for recognition of creative goods within existing trade agreements. However, there has been a growing consensus over the last few years that the best way to deal with this matter would be via a convention covering international trade in the cultural sector – one that emphasised the need for preserving cultural diversity. One of the strongest calls for a cultural diversity convention has arisen precisely from this quarter.

Culture and globalisation
Further stimulus for such an international convention on cultural diversity arises from the widespread concern that globalisation, taken in its broadest sense, is a threat to people's sense of their own cultural identity. There is no doubt that this fear has been an important factor mobilising 'anti-globalisation' protests around the world, where banners often proclaim the United States or transnational corporations as villains seeking to impose a homogenised culture on everything and everyone. In such

demonstrations a number of different targets and problems are often conflated and purposes may easily become blurred. Nevertheless there is no denying the depth of apprehension among the participants about where the world seems to be heading.

It is clear that the breakdown of barriers to flows of capital and labour between countries, the rise of the internet, the growing internationalisation of markets, the fall of communism and the emergence of the United States as a global superpower – all aspects of 'globalisation' – have contributed each in their own way to redefining how we live. The adoption of new communications technologies means that cultural messages and symbols are being transmitted in volumes and at speeds that have never been witnessed before. In many cases the messages and symbols are associated with consumer products which, as they penetrate markets more and more widely scattered around the world, carry with them an inevitable sense of standardisation. It is not just the familiar images conveyed by global corporate branding, but also the more complex cultural content conveyed by television programmes or the songs of popular music performers that contribute to this feeling that we are living in an increasingly homogenised environment.

However, the evidence on the cultural impact of globalisation is mixed, particularly because these are dynamic processes in a constant state of evolution. If impact is measured by the observable spread of universally recognised cultural symbols as described above, certainly some homogenisation has occurred. And, to the extent that a majority of such symbols have originated in the USA, it is understandable that such a process is seen as 'Americanisation', a perception that can only be heightened by the seemingly relentless economic and military dominance of the United States in the post-millennium world. Nevertheless, the very threat of external cultural influences may actually sharpen the resolve of particular groups, be they local communities or nation states, to assert their own cultural distinctiveness. Indeed, there is little indication that cultural differentiation within or between countries is dying out. The celebration of specific cultural identities through art, music, literature, ritual, tradition and in many other ways is clearly alive and well in all parts of the world. One only has to tune in to the local television station in an Indonesian village, or attend a funeral in Mexico, watch a Russian circus performance, or visit a Japanese shrine – to be convinced that there is no such thing as a standard global culture.

Furthermore, globalisation has many positive impacts on cultural diversity. New communications technologies provide unprecedented opportunities for intercultural dialogue, enabling a rich range of cultural influences to be accessed at the click of a mouse. In addition, much innovation in artistic production has been stimulated by the development of new media, giving artists an expanded kit of tools with which to work, and consumers a plethora of new and exciting experiences.

Nevertheless, dark shadows persist: the fear of cultural domination and loss of identity, the pressure of forces that people feel unable to control. These effects, vaguely ascribed to globalisation, have helped to prompt the idea of a convention to protect cultural diversity. Such an instrument, it is argued, could help us at least to distinguish the positive and negative impacts of globalisation, fostering the former while holding the latter at bay.

Culture and sustainable development

The third and final impetus towards a cultural diversity treaty that I want to discuss stems from a profound sense that countries of the Third World are losing out in the process of economic and cultural development.

The pre-eminence of industrialised countries in determining the way the global economy works and their domination of markets for cultural goods and services has exacerbated the economic and cultural disadvantage suffered by poorer countries. These problems are clearly related to the trade and globalisation issues discussed above. But the difficulty here is specific: the impacts both of liberalisation of trade in cultural goods and of globalisation processes more generally are felt in the developing world with particular severity. Cultural exports from the Third World are swallowed up in the global market place, while at the same time these countries have few resources to protect their own cultural diversity from the penetration of cultural influences originating beyond their borders. Hence some form of international agreement on cultural diversity could be one way of identifying the specific needs of these countries, and of proposing remedies.

A central concept in considering these issues is that of sustainability. It will be recalled that notions of sustainable development were first given policy substance through the work of the UN World Commission on Environment and Development (WCED), whose report *Our Common Future* (1987) articulated the links between Third World poverty, the environment, ecological systems and the economy. Subsequently the UN World Commission on Culture and Development (WCCD) proposed similar linkages for culture, advocating a reorientation of development thinking towards an acknowledgement of the centrality of culture in the economic development process. Since the publication of the WCCD report, appropriately titled *Our Creative Diversity* (1994), interest has grown in finding ways to promote economic and cultural development as complementary strategies for the developing world.

One way of doing so is to foster the growth of community-based cultural industries – small-scale enterprises making pottery and textiles, local radio and television production, music groups producing tapes and records through neighbourhood studios for local consumption, community newspapers and magazines telling the people's own stories, and so on. All of these activities use the tangible and intangible cultural capital specific to a village, town or region to produce goods and services that have both economic and cultural value. These forms of localised cultural production not only create employment and incomes for the community, they also help to maintain a sense of cultural identity and to nurture creativity, thereby serving the objectives of both economic and cultural development.

It is not difficult to reconcile the pursuit of culturally sustainable development with the protection and enhancement of cultural diversity. It has become apparent that an international convention could be one way of facilitating these processes, especially if such a convention were to require rich countries to provide development assistance and other forms of co-operation and support to the less well-off nations of the world, to help them protect and promote their own cultures.

Prospects for a treaty

It is easy enough to propose such an international convention: to make it happen is a little more difficult. First, the labyrinthine bureaucracies of the international civil service have to be cranked into gear. Then a process has to be set up that can reach agreement upon the content of a possible convention. Once a draft form of words has been proposed, 150 or so countries, which have a vote in the intergovernmental committee responsible for making a decision, must agree to it. Finally, when the terms of a convention are ultimately endorsed, countries still have to sign up, and many are likely to find reasons for not doing so.

Nevertheless, despite the obstacles, the process is under way. A draft text for a *Convention on the Protection of the Diversity of Cultural Contents and Artistic Expressions* has been prepared by an independent committee of experts (known in the impenetrable jargon of UNESCO as a 'Category VI' committee). This text will be considered by a 'Category II' committee of government representatives, and no doubt by a host of other committees of indeterminate category, before it reaches the General Conference of UNESCO in late 2005. If all goes according to plan during this lengthy gestation, a brand new UN convention on cultural diversity may well be born by the end of next year.

The draft convention that is now on the table addresses a number of the issues I have discussed in this paper. It affirms the rights of countries to formulate cultural policies to foster creative expression and to promote the positive aspects of cultural diversity within a context of respect for fundamental human rights and freedoms. It pays particular attention to the need for sustainable cultural and economic development, and proposes mechanisms for international co-operation and solidarity. It deals with threats to cultural diversity, however they might arise, by requiring countries to take protective action if vulnerable forms of cultural expression are in danger of extinction or serious curtailment. Whether these proposals will be acceptable, and equal to the task of resolving the problems of cultural trade, remains to be seen.

Is it likely that the contemporary state of the world will be receptive to exhortations that we all have to live together in harmony if humankind is to have a future? At a time when fundamentalists of many different sorts are becoming more strident in their assertions that they are right and everyone else is wrong, and are seeking more and more strongly to persuade or coerce others to their way of thinking, even the neutral virtue of tolerance seems a long way off. In these circumstances the Utopian vision of the draft UNESCO treaty may seem an unrealisable dream. Yet human beings have always found that dreams are essential to seeing the way forward. And we can draw some hope from the fact that the best dreamers are artists – writers, painters, musicians, clowns and storytellers; all those who engage the creative life and who rescue the poetry of civilisation for us all to see and hear. They are the ones, wherever they come from, who can teach us not just to accept difference, but to celebrate it as a rich and positive aspect of the human condition.

Further reading

Jerry V. Diller, *Cultural Diversity: a Primer for the Human Services* (2nd edn), Belmont CA: Thomson, Brooks/Cole, 2004.

Mary E. Footer and Christoph Beat Graber, 'Trade liberalisation and cultural policy', *Journal of International Economic Law*, 3 (1), March 2000: 115–44.

R. D. Grillo, *Pluralism and the Politics of Difference: State, Culture and Ethnicity in Comparative Perspective*, Oxford: The Clarendon Press, 1998.

Monica Shelley and Margaret Winck (eds), *Aspects of European Cultural Diversity*, London: Routledge, 1993.

Katérina Stenou (ed.), *Universal Declaration on Cultural Diversity*, Paris: UNESCO, 2002.

David Throsby, *Economics and Culture*, Cambridge: Cambridge University Press, 2001.

UNESCO, *Cultural Diversity, Conflict and Pluralism* (World Culture Report 2000), Paris: UNESCO, 2000.

World Commission on Culture and Development, *Our Creative Diversity*, Paris: UNESCO, 1994.

Culture: merchandise or an ideal/value?

Issiaka-Prosper Lalèyê

In this day and age, we recognise cultural diversity and declare that it is an intrinsic good.[1] We want to protect the diversity of cultural content and artistic expression by adopting a universal declaration. Let us consider the conception and drafting of such a legal tool as an opportunity for various levels of reflection, analysis, and decision-making.

How shall we define culture and cultural diversity? What makes both important? Further questions arise above and beyond definition: the adherence of signatory states; what will enable them to attain the objectives set out in any declaration; how to deal with any breaches or violations; partnerships between non-governmental organisations and signatory states; the resolution of conflicts between the various stakeholders wishing to enforce the declaration – to mention just a few.

Determining whether culture is of commercial or some other kind of value can be considered as both a starting point and a common thread for all these questions. We will never attain the objectives of a declaration on cultural diversity unless we can agree on a clear vision of diversity and on the belief that cultural diversity deserves to be recognised, protected, promoted, and defended as a value.

I want to examine the notion of cultural diversity more closely. Does this expression denote precise boundaries and distinct content? Does the same thinking apply to biodiversity as to cultural diversity? Does our idea of cultural diversity faithfully reflect the reality we would like to achieve? If we can answer these, we will be able to answer the question at the centre of this debate: is culture a tradeable commodity or a social and moral ideal/value?

Some definitions

Over and above dictionary definition, words are given much of their meaning by the many ways we use them on a daily basis. Word usage is the melting pot in which new meanings are continuously created. Words like *culture, diversity, biodiversity*, and many other related expressions are no exception.

When we talk or think about culture, our experience can take any of three forms: sensory, intellectual, and practical. Theories of culture are an intellectual attempt to embrace and circumscribe such cultural experience. We have to admit that our cultural theory is lagging far behind our cultural experience as the 21st century gets under way.

It was at the end of the 19th century that theoreticians, ethnologists and anthropologists alike first began trying to grasp and more adequately define what is meant by 'culture'. Theoreticians from Tylor (1870)[2] to Lévi-Strauss (1949) made a sustained effort to construct a theory of culture as a unified and distinct object of knowledge. One of their major conclusions was that 'culture' is not based on our biological make-up, but rather on our belonging to a group, that is, a society. Culture, unlike instinct, is essentially transmitted non-automatically, which is why education and a prolonged childhood are so important for us compared with animals. The concept of a culture may be primarily used not to distinguish one individual from another individual, so much as one group of individuals from another group. How then do we distinguish humans from other humans? This century-long effort at definition remains unfinished and therefore imperfect from a number of points of view.[3]

Let us take three of the characteristic limitations of such thinking to date, in an age moreover marked by a gargantuan melding of cultures. First, the distinction between culture and nature may lead us to overlook the ways in which culture, while not being subject to the laws of nature as such, may also have its own nature which only a true theory of culture, or culturology, can encompass. Second, our current idea of culture does not allow us to determine which parts of everything culture represents take precedence as a root or source for its other parts. Religion, philosophy, science, ethics, politics, arts, and technology are all so important to a given culture and are each representative of the whole of that culture. But are they interchangeable? If we were able to describe culture the way Descartes described philosophy when he said that it is like a tree whose roots are metaphysics, whose trunk is physics, and whose three main branches are mechanics, medicine, and ethics, we would be closer to determining how to approach cultural diversity without compromising the authenticity of any particular culture. We would be more secure in our promotion of the diversity of cultures on a more or less conscious level, and in a more or less voluntary way.

Last, our current theory of culture draws heavily on the premise that culture is to society what personality is to the individual. This parallel between individual/psyche (or personality) and society/mentality (or culture), while rarely clearly formulated, is nevertheless present throughout the history of ethnoanthropology, from Tylor and Morgan to Lévi-Strauss. In the sociology of knowledge, indeed, it constitutes one of the basic tenets. Simple and useful as it is, however, it leads to certain problems in dealing with the co-existence of today's societies and their cultures. We know for a fact that individuals are capable of a renewal of being which is not adequately described in terms of personality simply being projected on to the screen of time. However, we persist in thinking that cultures which are being lost in the whirlwind of multiple interchanges – a phenomenon that is singularly accelerated in our era – can only protect their authenticity by respecting their traditions.[4]

In short, our current theory of culture, as handed down to us by the field of ethnoanthropology with all the trappings of scientific respectability, tells us little more than who the producer is. We are incapable of explaining by which mechanisms (much less by which laws), and for what reasons, a given culture spreads, and we cannot begin to understand the impact of the multitude of intrusions caused by the incessant and increasingly numerous exchanges that are occurring at an ever-accelerating pace.

Cultural diversity

The notion of cultural diversity rests entirely on the notion of difference, which supposes a comparison generally resulting from a judgment based on an observation, or evaluation. In mathematics, everyone can see that 3 is different from 5. Everyone also agrees that the difference is equal to 2. This is a quantitative difference that is easy to measure, and that is likely to be accepted by all. The same is not true for qualitative differences. While they are easy to observe most of the time, they are often difficult to express, and judgments are rarely unanimous. Even when such a consensus is reached, it is practically impossible to assess accurately the content. Thus, when two people agree that a dish that they have just tasted is good, or even excellent, they have no idea how the other person really experienced it.

Both inside and outside culture, everything seems to rest on qualitative differences. Cultural diversity is nothing more than this subtle, complex, more or less vast, and more or less fathomable difference that characterises cultures, whether we examine them individually, in relation to others, in space, or in time. Looking at it from this angle, stating that cultural diversity in and of itself deserves to be recognised, proclaimed, and protected, is a leap of faith. It assumes that our judgments and our choices carry more weight than our knowledge. This is why the problem of developing a standard-setting tool to regulate interactions between human societies and their cultures requires calm reflection, taking fully into consideration what we want and what we know, before we act.

Cultural diversity and biodiversity

Natural and cultural diversity share many points in common. The first point in common between these two diversities is the numerical immensity of the material objects and ideals and their differences each connotes. The second point they have in common is the permanence of this diversity or, in other words, the continual and apparently uninterrupted nature of the differences that are expressed or exteriorised. Both forms of diversity become more manageable if these differentiations can be grouped into large categories. This makes it possible to talk of families and sub-families or, using the more rigorous terminology developed by Aristotle nearly 25 centuries ago, genera, species, individuals, specific differences, and so forth. Humankind early seized on the classificatory method so that we might organise what we knew into 'capsules' of knowledge, which would accord us power over nature, and power over humankind itself.

However, natural diversity differs from cultural diversity in a number of ways. Biodiversity appears given or offered, while cultural diversity appears to be manufactured. Man is the wellspring of the differences expressed inside and outside cultures, while it is God the Creator, or some natural force for those who do not believe in the existence of God, that is the wellspring of the continual, inexhaustible differences seen in nature. Consequently, the main difference between the diversity of nature and the diversity of culture is that the first is a product of necessity while the second is partly that and partly a product of freedom, more precisely, of human freedom: the actions of individuals and/or societies whose distinctive trait, thanks to our individual and collective conscience, is the ability to think.

Culture: tradeable commodity or a social and moral ideal/value?
If, in our day and age, we are raising this question, it is because we are living in a period of sweeping intermingling. Globalisation, which is running its course before our very eyes, is mainly about exchanges. We would like to be able to buy and sell everything. Those 'merchants' who see culture as simply merchandise would like to see the rules of the marketplace apply to everything produced

and traded by humankind. Their opponents call for a modicum of discrimination to protect culture from these global exchanges.

Paradoxically, both are right. This is why we must continue to examine the main issues that have been obscured and repressed by our current way of thinking about culture. Then we can turn to the function of exchange and the marketplace in the context of a society tied to a culture, and address ourselves to the ultimate reason for its existence.

Questions that are obscured and repressed

These areas of questioning fall conveniently into Aristotle's four categories of causality: material, formal, efficient and final:

- Cultural material. What is the raw material of culture? No material can be excluded from culture. In the past, we have always separated the material from the spiritual. But given the enormous number of cultures and the numerous differences that characterise them today, the human spirit of course, but also maybe the spirits of the gods – and even the Holy Spirit which inspire cultures – need to be taken into account. Meanwhile, nature must also be considered as a raw material of culture. Do cultures process such a broad range of materials in the same way? If so, why are they so different? And what distinguishes one way from the others? So complex are these questions that we would rather simply affirm that cultures are different and that it is just and good that it should be this way. But what are the consequences of this naïve optimism?
- Cultural form. Society is the wellspring of many different forms of culture. Religion, philosophy, science, ethics, art, and technology may all be considered forms of culture. But how many are there? Do we already know them all? If not, which ones might yet be discovered? And what are the relationships between these forms? Gaining a better understanding of these

relationships may also help us understand what impact they have both on the home culture to which they belong, and those cultures that are foreign to them but that history forces them either to be subsumed into or to incorporate. Most sincere champions of cultural diversity regard it as natural and even desirable that religions expand their influence beyond the regions from which they originate, and that science, technology, and more recently international development and democracy, are accessible to as many societies as possible. However, these forms of culture may only penetrate distant cultures on a superficial level. Religion, philosophy, science and technology can only be said to be forms of culture 'equally' present in all cultures in a formal sense. Materially speaking, their impact differs enormously from culture to culture. The spread of some to all societies regardless can only be to the detriment of cultural diversity. The fact that these questions are bewildering and that their implications are destabilising should not deter us from posing them. Repressing them will result only in unproductive contradictions, leading to a dead-end.

- Cultural effects. The excessively materialistic conception we have of culture inevitably encourages us to consider it as a product of society. Without saying anything openly, this assumes that societies can produce only their own culture. Such spontaneous beliefs regarding culture prevent us from seeing the myriad ways in which cultural elements in today's neighbouring and coexisting societies are continuously undergoing exchange, at an ever-increasing speed. What this illustrates in turn is the enormous potential of societies to extend beyond the geographical limits of their cultures. What are the effects on cultures of the exogenous elements that continuously pour in from other cultures? Since it is evident that these elements cannot fail to have an impact, what is the threshold at which they may be deemed to provoke qualitative change in the 'host culture'? To cite just one case, for a number of centuries, black African cultures have been subjected to the growing influence of European cultures. With acculturation well under way, when will these African cultures stop being African? What will they then become? Can there be a final answer to such a question, apart from the final form such a culture takes?

- Culture's final purpose. Let us suppose that the 'betterment' of humankind and society is the purpose the Creator has given to his creation. What are the consequences of such a supposition on the way we conceive culture and cultural diversity? If, as modern biology leads us to believe, species are continuously disappearing from nature so that natural diversity is becoming increasingly impoverished, what about cultural diversity? Do the differences between human cultures have to narrow for humankind to better itself? Or, on the contrary, do these differences have to become more pronounced to ensure that humankind and society improve far beyond what they are today? As long as we do not know the ultimate goal of the creation of humankind and society, we will be unable to say whether cultural diversity will help or hinder the attainment of this goal. Since religions are different from one another, which one of them should we believe in? Has the trend among religions to set themselves apart as unique entities – a process that mirrors other forms of culture – already given rise to the 'best' religion, or is that still to come? Humankind, like societies, is capable of taking action. Has sociology finished revealing the subtle but effective ways that individual actions can amalgamate with collective actions to lead us inexorably towards a goal of which we remain unaware?

It must be said, looking at these groups based on Aristotle's four modes of causality, that our current conception of culture and cultural diversity contains more unknowns than knowns. So how should we respond to the most urgent given of our contemporary world: the impact of global trade on our experience of culture and cultural diversity?

Exchange, the marketplace, and culture

The interrelations that characterise the lives of humans living in societies can all be reduced to the fundamental idea of exchanges: exchanging words, ideas, feelings, goods, and services, as well as, up to a certain point, exchanging exchanges themselves. Exchanges are thus the driving force in intrasocial and intersocial interrelations. It is not surprising then that cultures have been marked in so many ways by them. As relations between societies grow in number and complexity, exchanges reveal to what extent they are a determining factor in the survival of societies and their cultures. Physical or virtual, but always real, the marketplace is nothing more than the space where these exchanges take place.

Exchanges between the different forms of a given culture are indispensable and irreplaceable and, for all intents and purposes, vital. Both within and without a culture, they are the true cause of diversity and the true driving force of diversification. This is why we cannot deal with cultural diversity without considering its relationship to the marketplace. The current era is characterised by a marketplace that is already globalised and whose interrelations are strengthening and accelerating.

However, this centrality of the phenomenon of exchange with respect to culture and cultural diversity does not preclude a certain resistance to widespread exchanges. The challenge we are faced with is how not to turn our backs on all exchanges, but to classify them into categories that guide and serve as a reliable foundation for our individual and collective choices. This is where we are justified in turning to our social and moral ideals for guidance. This is where the marketplace needs to be brought into line with our broadest conception of the value of culture and cultural diversity.

Selling and buying are not the only forms of exchange between humans and societies. Giving is also a form of exchange, as is lending. There are forms of sharing that are neither selling, nor buying, nor giving, nor lending, but that none the less contribute to interrelations between humans. Any reflection on culture and cultural diversity forces us to step outside the narrow paradigm of selling, buying, and lending to rediscover the gifts of giving and sharing.

In the specific forms of exchange represented by selling and buying, especially if we limit ourselves to a material object, the object exchanged is *totally* sold and *totally* bought. However, as the object at the centre of the exchange becomes less and less material, it becomes difficult or even impossible to sell it or buy it totally. The music that a musician may be paid to produce will be consumed at the same time by the buyer and the seller, but it may also be consumed by an audience of neither buyers nor sellers. While the buyer of a picture painted by an artist can leave with it and be the only one to enjoy it, we know very well that, as the buyer, he cannot possess the image of the picture carried in the artist's mind. We know that it is a picture that he is buying. He cannot buy the artist's skill at painting pictures.

Without losing its function as both a virtual and real space where exchange takes place, a marketplace can be a place for exchanges that are not solely selling and buying or lending and repaying. The deep protective emotion that we feel when we think of culture and cultural diversity today is not a desire for a pure and simple expulsion of culture from the space where exchanges occur.

Conclusion

If we consider the obscured and repressed questions that we have touched on above, our current conception of culture may appear naïve. However, as we attempt to find answers to these questions, we will arrive at a more faithful conception of culture based on our real experience – one that is less naïve, more critical, and more aware of the limits of our understanding. At this stage, we can sum up three main aspects of the reality of culture that our current conception tends to repress or omit. The first mistake is to confuse culture as a whole with only one of its components, namely art. The second is to consider culture as a product, while ignoring the producer and the production process as a whole. The third is to see culture as a desirable form of merchandise in and of itself, when we do not know its ultimate purpose.

What we do know, meanwhile, is that the different forms of culture do not conform in the normal way to the rules of trade. Notwithstanding the ideal nature of saints and gods, objects of worship and articles of devotion are exchanged everywhere for money without shaking the faith of believers. The lofty ideal of justice does not prevent judges and lawyers from asking their clients to pay for their services. The fact that science is devoted solely to the truth does not prevent technological discoveries from being sold.

We know also that considering culture as a range of products but neglecting its producers has an unfortunate impact on our current conception of culture, because it tricks us into thinking that what we can do with the product we can also do with its maker. Thus, for example, we think that the product of an artistic activity can be exchanged for money (and, of course, if the selling of art were prohibited, artists would die of hunger). But if one wants to promote a culture, it is not enough to have regard simply to the art it produces. One must also be able to define the culture in its entirety (art being included within this remit), so as to find a way of protecting it against the irreversible trivialisation that results from an unthinking surrender to market forces.

Ignoring, even unintentionally, the mechanisms that produce a culture, has an even more pernicious, effect, in my opinion. Human societies give the impression that they produce their cultures as naturally as the liver produces bile. Unfortunately, this is a deceptive image. All evidence points to the complexity of the mechanisms that produce a culture. The transmission of culture through apprenticeships, education, initiation or in a single word, 'enculturation' – the term coined by Tylor in 1870 – are clearly the direction to look in. Modern research conducted by anthropologists interested in basic personality has only served to strengthen Tylor's emphasis on the subtlety of these mechanisms.

What is certain is that when we introduce a new system of human education into a society, regardless of the supposed merits of the new system, it will have a profound impact on the mechanisms of production and reproduction of its culture. The homogenisation, whether conscious or unconscious, of humankind's current cultures by the protagonists of globalisation inevitably constitutes a fundamental attack against the protection of the authenticity of culture and of cultural diversity.

Meanwhile, the answer to the question of our title can only be nuanced. With respect to culture as a form of production, with respect to the producer of the culture, and with respect to the mechanisms that produce and reproduce the culture, the final answer cannot yet be formulated. However, the simple act of asking the question is a sign of hope – as Karl Marx once said: 'Mankind thus inevitably sets itself only such tasks as it is able to solve.' [5]

Endnotes

[1] UNESCO *Universal Declaration on Cultural Diversity: a Vision, a Conceptual Platform, a Pool of Ideas for Implementation, a New Paradigm*, Cultural Diversity Series, No. 1, Paris, 2003, p. 64.

[2] E. B. Tylor, *Primitive culture*, 1871.

[3] Issiaka-Prosper Lalèyê, *Comment meurent les cultures*, notably beginning on p. 283.

[4] Issiaka-Prosper Lalèyê, *De la genèse traditionelle de la philosophie aux fonctions philosophiques de la pensée dans les traditions négroafricaines actualles*, Revue Sénégalaise de Philosophie, No. 15/16, January 1992, pp. 119–37.

[5] K. Marx, cited by Raymond Aron, *Les étapes de la pensée sociologique*, p. 153.

Further reading

Aron R., *Les étapes de la pensée sociologique*, Paris, Gallimard, 1967, pp. 664.

Chalmers Alan F., *Qu'est-ce que la science? Récents développements en philosophie des sciences: Popper, Kuhn, Lakatos, Feyerabend*, translated from the English (What is This Thing Called Science?: An Assessment of the Nature and Status of Science and Its Methods) by Michel Biezunski, Editions La Découverte, Paris, 1988, p. 236.

Copans J. & M. Godelier, *L'anthropologie? Sciences des sociétés primitives? Le point de la question*, Paris, ed. Ep. Denoël, 1971, p. 310.

Cowen T., *Creative Destruction, How globalization is changing the world's cultures*, Princeton University Press, Princeton, New Jersey, 2002, p. 180.

_____, *In Praise of Commercial Culture*, Cambridge, Harvard University Press, 1998.

Issiaka-Prosper Lalèyê, 'Comment meurent les cultures? Interrogations philosophico-anthropologiques sur le concept de génocide culturel', dans Boustany Katia et Dormoy Daniel (under the direction of), *GENOCIDE(S)*, Collection de Droit International, Publications du Réseau Vitoria, Editions Bruylant., Editions de l'Université de Bruxelles, 1999, pp. 265–93.

_____, 'En deçà de l'idéologie du développement et du culte de la culture' » dans ETHIOPIQUES, Revue Négro-africaine de Littérature et de Philosophie, No. 62, 1er trimestre 1999, Dakar, Fondation Léopold Sédar Senghor, 1999, pp. 103–10.

_____, 'Le même et l'autre de l'homme. Le savoir aux prises avec la différence' dans Philosophies africaines: traversées des expériences, *Rue Descartes n°36*, Collège International de Philosophie, June 2002, Paris, Presses Universitaires de France, pp. 75–91.

_____, 'Humanismes et idéologies du développement. La contemporanéité à l'épreuve de l'essentiel humain', dans *Humanismos latinos em Africa: encontros et desencontros*, Actes du Colloque International de Dakar, 9–11 January 2003, Fondatione Cassamarca, Treviso, 2003, pp. 161–75.

Laplantine François, *L'anthropologie*, Paris, Payot, 2001 (1st edn 1987), p. 244.

McLean G. F. & Kromkowski (eds), *Relations between cultures*, Cultural Heritage and Contemporary Change, Series I. Culture and Values, Vol. 4, The Council for Research in Values and Philosophy, Washington, DC, 1991, pp. 396.

Singleton, Mike, 'De l'épaississement empirique à l'interpellation interprétative en passant par l'ampliation analogique: une méthode pour l'anthropologie prospective', in *Recherches sociologiques*, Volume XXXII, No. 1, 2001, pp. 15–40.

Contributors

Jean-Michel Baer became a member of the Cabinet of Jacques
Delors, the President of the European Commission, in 1985. He had
charge of social issues, cultural, news radio communications, and
television policies. From 1994 to 2003, he was Director of Audio-
visual (including educational and cultural multimedia), Cultural and
Sports Policy at the European Commission's Directorate-General for
Education and Culture. He is currently special adviser to the
president of Arte, and a member of an independent study circle
sponsored by *Le Monde* and the French political science Institute,
Sciences Po, Paris, to reflect upon issues relating to the cinema
(political, legal, technical, economic and aesthetic), commission
research to this end, and publish the results. This group is called
'L'Exception'. See also 'L'exception culturelle. Une règle en quête de
contenus', initially published in *En Temps Réel*, no.11, October 2003
www.entempsreel.org

Arjo Klamer has held the chair in the Economics of Art and Culture
at Erasmus University Rotterdam, since 1994. After graduating in
1977, he pursued his PhD in economics at Duke University. His
articles about cultural contrasts between the USA and Europe were
published by KLM in 1989. Arjo's most recent book is *The Value of
Culture: On the Relationship between Economics and the Arts*
(Amsterdam University Press, 1996). Recognition came with the
publication of *Conversations with Economists* (Rowman and
Allanheld, 1983), named by *Business Week* as among the 'ten best
business books of the year'. He is currently writing a book about the
peculiarities of economists and their discipline. Affiliated with George
Washington University as a research professor, Arjo Klamer is
involved in two theatre companies and a museum in the Netherlands,
where he lives with his wife and four children.

David Throsby is internationally known for his work in the economics of the arts and culture. His book, *The Economics of the Performing Arts*, co-authored with Glenn Withers and first published in 1979, has become a standard reference work in the field. In addition to the performing arts, his research and writing has covered the economic role of artists, the economics of public intervention in arts markets, cultural development, cultural policy, heritage issues, and sustainability of cultural processes. His most recent book, *Economics and Culture*, published in 2001 by Cambridge University Press, bases its arguments on a foundation of theories of value and develops the twin notions of economic and cultural value as underlying principles for integrating the two fields. David Throsby has been Professor of Economics at Macquarie University in Sydney since 1974, and a consultant to many government organisations, as well as the World Bank, the OECD, the Food and Agriculture Organization of the United Nations and UNESCO.

Issiaka-Prosper Lalèyê, has been professor of Epistemology and Anthropology in the Sociology Department of Gaston Berger University, in Saint-Louis (Sénégal) since 1990. He was editor-in-chief of the university's multidisciplinary review, *Université, Recherche et Développement* from 1993 to 2003. Born in Benin in 1942, he gained his PhD in 1970 in the University of Fribourg, and a state Doctorate in Arts and Social Sciences in the Sorbonne in 1988. He has written many articles on African philosophy, teaching philosophy in Africa and philosophy in general; anthropology and African religions and religious experience; Yoruba thought; and the foundations for democracy and scientific advance in Africa. Professor Lalèyê was a member of the group of independent experts (Category VI) who prepared, at Director-General Matsuura's request, a first draft of the UNESCO International *Convention on the Protection of the Diversity of Cultural Contents and Artistic Expressions*. He is married with five children.

Fiona Bartels-Ellis is Head of Equality Opportunity and Diversity at the British Council and has global responsibility for its equal opportunity and diversity work. Her approach aims to ensure that this work is premised on mainstreaming and linked to cultural relations. In addition, Fiona is leading the British Council's work on corporate social responsibility. Fiona who joined the British Council in March 2000 from the University of Westminster, where she led its Master's in Advanced Social Work Programme, very much wants to make a lasting contribution to developing a fairer, more tolerant and inclusive organisational culture and has a particular interest in mediation. Fiona has a background in social work where anti-oppressive practice was central to her work. For 20 years she combined social work education with freelance consultancy in the field of equal opportunity and diversity. She is an accredited practitioner of the Higher Education Academy and supports voluntary initiatives in Ghana, where she was born.